MW01617736

THE LION, THE
AND THE WARDROBE

Written by C. S. Lewis

Teacher Guide

Leigh Lowe & Brett Vaden

www.MemoriaPress.com

THE LION, THE WITCH AND THE WARDROBE
Written by C. S. Lewis

TEACHER GUIDE
Leigh Lowe & Brett Vaden

ISBN 9781615380534

First Edition © 2010 Memoria Press 0117

Cover illustration by Starr Steinbach

All rights reserved. No part of this book may be reproduced in any form by any means without written permission from the publisher.

Contents

PREPARING TO READ:

REVIEW

- Orally review any previous vocabulary.
- Review the plot of the book as read so far.
- Periodically review the concepts of character, setting, and plot.

STUDY GUIDE PREVIEW

- Reading Notes:
  - Read aloud together
  - This section gives the students key characters, places, terms that are relevant to a particular time period, etc.
- Vocabulary:
  - Read aloud together so that students will recognize words when they come across them in their reading.
- Comprehension Questions:
  - Read through these questions with students to encourage purposeful reading.

READING:

- Student reads the chapter (or selection of the chapter for that lesson) independently or to the teacher (for younger students).
- For younger students, you can alternate between teacher-read and student-read passages. Model good reading skills. Encourage students to read expressively and smoothly. Teacher may occasionally take oral reading grades.
- While reading, mark each vocabulary word as you come across it.
- Have students take note in their study guide margin of pages where a comprehension question is answered.

AFTER READING:

VOCABULARY

- Look at each word within the context that it is used, and help your students come up with the best synonym that defines the word. (Make sure students know the meaning of the synonym.)
- Record the word's meaning in the students' study guides. (Use students' knowledge of Latin and other vocabulary to decipher meanings.)

COMPREHENSION QUESTIONS

- Older students can answer these questions independently, but younger students (2nd-4th) need to answer the questions orally, form a good sentence, and then write it down, using correct punctuation, capitalization, and spelling. (You may want to write the sentence down for younger students after forming it orally, and then let students copy it perfectly.)
- It is not necessary to write the answer to every question. Some may be better answered orally.
- Answering questions and composing answers is a valuable learning activity. Questions require students to think; writing a concise answer is a good composition exercise.

QUOTATIONS AND DISCUSSION QUESTIONS

- Use the Quotations and Discussion Questions section of each lesson as a guide to your oral discussion of the key concepts in the chapter that may not be covered in the comprehension questions.
- These talking points can take your oral discussion to a higher level than covered in the students' written work. Use this time as an opportunity to introduce higher-level thinking. You can introduce concepts the students may not be mature enough to fully understand yet but that would be beneficial for them to begin thinking about.
- A key to the Discussion Questions is in the back of the Teacher Guide.

ENRICHMENT

- The Enrichment activities include composition, copywork, dictation, research, mapping, drawing, poetry work, literary terms, and more.
- This section has a variety of activities in it, but the most valuable activity is composition. Your students should complete at least one composition assignment each week. Proof students' work and have students copy composition until grammatically perfect. Insist on clear, concise writing. For younger students, start with 2-3 sentences, and do the assignment together. The students can form good sentences orally as you write them down, and then the students copy them.
- These activities can be completed as time and interest allow. Do not feel you need to complete all of these activities. Choose the ones that you feel are the best use of your students' time.

UNIT REVIEW AND TESTS

- There is a unit review and a quiz or test following every few lessons (varies by individual guide).
- On the weeks that have these reviews and tests, you may want to do the review early in the week, and then drill it orally a couple of times before giving the test at the end of the week.
- A final comprehensive test is also included.

Introduction

C. S. Lewis was born in Belfast, Northern Ireland, in 1898. His childhood was a sad one. When he was ten years old his mother died, and in that same year his father sent him to a boarding school he did not care for. His older brother Warren attended school with him, which proved comforting. After two years the school closed and Lewis returned to attend a school about a mile from his father's home. As a boy, perhaps to overcome some of his sadness, Lewis immersed himself in literature, particularly the stories of Beatrix Potter (author of *Peter Rabbit*), and mythology. He also loved animals; he even created his own imaginary world with talking animals called Boxen. These childhood interests followed Lewis through life and are evident in his *Chronicles of Narnia* books.

As he grew up, C. S. Lewis was an avid reader and a good student. He eventually won a scholarship to Oxford University in England. A year after he enrolled, he joined the British Army and fought in World War I. After the war ended, he returned to Oxford to study literature. He eventually became a tutor and a fellow at Oxford University, and professor of Medieval and Renaissance Literature at Cambridge University. During his career, he became close friends with J. R. R. Tolkien (author of *The Lord of the Rings* series). Tolkien was one of the first people to read and offer Lewis comments on *The Lion, the Witch and the Wardrobe*, the first of the Narnia books to be published, but which takes place second chronologically in the series. It was first published in 1950.

During his life, Lewis developed a reputation for being a great scholar and great defender of the Christian faith. He is considered one of the greatest Christian apologists of the twentieth century. (An apologist is one who argues in defense of an idea or belief.) In addition to writing the seven books in *The Chronicles of Narnia* series, Lewis wrote several books on the Christian faith during his lifetime. His most popular book is *Mere Christianity*, which began a series of radio addresses to the soldiers in World War II. *Mere Christianity* was voted best book of the twentieth century by *Christianity Today* magazine in 2000.

The topics and arguments in *Mere Christianity* are quite evident in *The Lion, the Witch and the Wardrobe* and the other Narnia books, which were written for Lewis' god-daughter. The Narnia books, though fantasy books for children, are also allegories of the Christian faith. (An allegory is a story that represents other events or ideas.) The characters and events in *The Lion, the Witch and the Wardrobe* clearly detail Biblical events and characters quite familiar to you. These representations will be discussed as you read.

C. S. Lewis died at the age of 64 on November 22, 1963. Though a great figure, Lewis' death was overshadowed by the assassination of President John F. Kennedy, which occurred on the same day.

Comprehension Questions

Answer the following in complete sentences.

1. Who is the author of *The Lion, the Witch and the Wardrobe*?
   C. S. Lewis is the author of *The Lion, the Witch and the Wardrobe.*
2. In what year was the book originally published? It was published in 1950.
3. How many books are there in *The Chronicles of Narnia* series? There are seven books in *The Chronicles of Narnia* series.
4. Where does *The Lion, the Witch and the Wardrobe* fit in the series sequence?
   It is the second book in the series sequence.
5. Where was the author born?
   C. S. Lewis was born in Belfast, Northern Ireland.
6. What famous university did the author attend? C. S. Lewis attended Oxford University.
7. The author taught English literature at which universities? C. S. Lewis was a professor of literature at the University of Oxford and the University of Cambridge.
8. Who was one of the author's best friends? What book did his friend write?
   J. R. R. Tolkien was one of his best friends. He wrote *The Lord of the Rings* series.
9. List two books the author was famous for writing.
   C. S. Lewis was famous for writing *The Chronicles of Narnia* and *Mere Christianity.*
10. For whom did the author write *The Lion, the Witch and the Wardrobe*?
    C. S. Lewis wrote the book for his god-daughter.
11. What is a Christian apologist?
    An apologist is one who argues in defense of an idea or belief; a Christian apologist proposes arguments in defense of Christianity.
12. What is an allegory?
    An allegory is a story that represents other events or ideas.
13. The author died on the same day as what historic event?
    The assassination of John F. Kennedy occurred on the same day as C. S. Lewis' death.

Reading Notes

air-raids attacks by fighter-planes and bombers
row argument
wardrobe a freestanding closet for hanging clothes
faun a creature with a man's body and goat's legs and horns

Vocabulary

Write the meaning of each bold word or phrase.

1. "This is very **queer**," she said strange
2. but she felt very **inquisitive** curious, or wanting to know more
3. he carried several brown-paper **parcels**. something wrapped up in paper; packages

Comprehension Questions

Answer the following in complete sentences.

1. List the children and identify the youngest.
Lucy is the youngest, then Edmund, Susan, and Peter.

2. Why were the children sent to the Professor's home in the country? During World War II, the city of London was heavily bombed. The children there were sent to live with families in the country, where it was less dangerous.

3. Describe the Professor's home and its setting. The Professor's home is large with long, winding passageways and rows of doors. The house is in the heart of the country, ten miles from the nearest railroad station and two miles from the nearest post office.

4. What does Lucy discover as she travels through the wardrobe? Lucy first discovers two rows of fur coats, but as she continues, she finds herself in the middle of a snow-covered wood at nighttime.

5. How does Lucy know she has entered a very different world on the other side of the wardrobe?
The first "person" Lucy meets is a faun, who looks like a man from the waist up, but has the legs, hoofs, tail, and horns of a goat.

Quotation

This story is about something that happened to them when they were sent away from London during the war because of the air-raids.

Discussion Questions

1. Read the second sentence of the chapter, quoted above. What can you deduce from this sentence?
2. Compare the Faun to the satyrs and nymphs of *D'Aulaires' Book of Greek Myths*.
3. Discuss the significance of the lamppost.
4. Can you think of other stories in which children travel to other worlds?

Enrichment

1. Look at the map of the British Isles in the Appendix. Observe and describe the different countries of this area, which is also called the United Kingdom.

   The United Kingdom, located in the North Sea, consists of the countries of England, Wales, Scotland, Ireland, and Northern Ireland. London is the capital of the United Kingdom.

   Draw a house plan of the Professor's home based on the description in the book.
2. Copy or write from dictation the first sentence in the last full paragraph of the chapter.

   He was only a little taller than Lucy herself and he carried over his head an umbrella, white with snow.

Reading Notes

melancholy	sad, depressed
jollification	merrymaking; festivity
handkerchief	small cloth used for wiping nose or face
cloven hoof	hoof divided or split into two

Vocabulary

Write the meaning of each bold word or phrase.

1. if only I had worked harder at **geography** the study of places on a map
2. put a **kettle** on. metal pot for boiling water or cooking
3. meet a poor **innocent** child in the wood not guilty of a crime

Comprehension Questions

Answer the following in complete sentences.

1. How does Tumnus tempt Lucy into coming with him? Tumnus tempts Lucy with a roaring fire, toast, sardines, and cake after she has initially declined his offer to join him for tea.
2. Describe Tumnus' home and how Lucy feels there. Tumnus lives in a little, dry, clean cave. It is well decorated and homey. Lucy thinks she has never been in a nicer place.
3. What does Tumnus confess after getting to know Lucy better? Tumnus confesses that he is a kidnapper for the White Witch and has lured Lucy, intending to turn her over to the Witch.
4. How does Tumnus redeem himself? Tumnus redeems himself by telling Lucy that he risked his fate to return her safely to the lamppost.
5. What memento does Lucy leave with Tumnus? Lucy gives Tumnus a handkerchief to keep as a memento.

Discussion Questions

1. Tumnus explains that it is always winter in Narnia. What feelings does winter evoke? Can you think of another story in which the seasons represent feelings?
2. Given the allegorical nature of the book, can you detect any Christian symbolism yet?
3. This chapter is flooded with references from mythology. List them.
4. Why do you think Narnia's eternal winter does not include Christmas?
5. List the books on Tumnus' shelf. What do they indicate about his interests?
   The books on Tumnus' shelf are *The Life and Letters of Silenus*; *Nymphs and Their Ways*; *Men, Monks, and Gamekeepers*; *A Study in a Popular Legend*; and *Is Man a Myth?* The books indicate that Tumnus is interested in humans and their relation to Fauns and the Creatures of the Wood.

Enrichment

1. Set Lucy sitting by the hearth in Mr. Tumnus' cave in a pencil sketch.
2. Locate Mr. Tumnus' cave on the Map of Narnia in the Appendix.
3. Who was Silenus in Greek mythology? Look up this name in an encyclopedia or mythology resource.
   He was the teacher and faithful companion of the wine-god Dionysus. He had special knowledge, wisdom, and powers of prophecy. Often he is depicted in satyr-like form.
4. Winter without Christmas would be dreary and disappointing. On the lines below, give two sentences that tell how it would be sad for you. Remember to indent, and use the first sentence of these directions as your topic sentence.

Reading Notes

heather low-growing flowering plant
sledge vehicle drawn by animals over snow
gilded covered with gold
champing their bits showing impatience; eager

Vocabulary

Write the meaning of each bold word or phrase.

1. a perfectly **ordinary** wardrobe. common, everyday kind
2. But it wasn't a **hoax** at all a trick to make something seem real that's not
3. He sneered and **jeered** at Lucy laughed scornfully at someone
4. proud and cold and **stern**. strict

Comprehension Questions

Answer the following in complete sentences.

1. What is unexpected about the time frame of Lucy's excursion in the wardrobe? Although Lucy has spent hours in Narnia with Mr. Tumnus, the others acts as though Lucy has only been out of their sight for a moment.
2. Why is Lucy miserable for several days following her adventure? Lucy is quite miserable upon returning from Narnia because her siblings think she is telling a silly lie.
3. Why does Lucy return to the wardrobe? After enduring the sneers and jeers of the others, especially Edmund, Lucy wants to return to the wardrobe to be sure her adventure had not been a dream.
4. Why does Edmund go into the wardrobe? Edmund follows Lucy into the wardrobe so he can continue to tease her about her "new country."
5. Describe the Queen of Narnia. The Queen is tall and covered in white fur. She carries a long golden wand. Her face is stark white, and she has a very red mouth. Her demeanor is proud, cold, and stern.

Quotation

She could have made it up with the others quite easily at any moment if she could have brought herself to say the whole thing was only a story made up for fun. But Lucy was a very truthful girl and she knew that she was really in the right; and she could not bring herself to say this.

Discussion Questions

1. Why do you think the author always tells us about the wardrobe door when the children enter Narnia?
2. Lucy shows great strength and conviction in this chapter. How do her actions represent a fundamental Christian ideal?
3. What is your reaction to the Queen of Narnia? How does the author's description of her make you feel?

Enrichment

1. Research satyrs, or fauns, again and find out if Mr. Tumnus acts like a true satyr as much as he looks like one. You can find a description of satyrs in *D'Aulaires Book of Greek Myths* in the entry about Pan.
2. Copy or write from dictation the first sentence of the paragraph after Mr. Tumnus says, "The whole wood is full of her spies. Even some of the trees are on her side." Try to place commas correctly.

   They both got up and left the tea things on the table, and Mr. Tumnus once more put up his umbrella and gave Lucy his arm, and they went out into the snow.

Reading Notes

mantle	loose, sleeveless cloak
Turkish Delight	jellylike cubes of candy covered in sugar
courtier	royal servant

Vocabulary

Write the meaning of each bold word or phrase.

1. And how, pray, did you come to enter my **dominions**? lands ruled by someone
2. this was **enchanted** Turkish Delight put under a spell
3. how **flushed** and strange his face was. red in the face; rose-cheeked

Comprehension Questions

Answer the following in complete sentences.

1. How does the Queen react when Edmund tells her he is a boy? The Queen is very inquisitive about how he entered Narnia and seems a little disturbed.

2. Describe the effect Turkish Delight has on Edmund. Once Edmund tastes the sweet softness of the Turkish Delight, he is hooked. He believes he has never tasted anything so delicious.

3. What promise does the Queen make to Edmund? The Queen tells Edmund that she is looking for a Prince to whom she can give her kingdom. She promises Edmund worldly prizes of wealth, power, etc.

4. What does Lucy learn during her second visit to Narnia? Lucy learns from Tumnus that the "Queen" is the White Witch, who took control without authority and has terrible magic powers that allow her to turn people into stone and that keep Narnia in a constant state of winter.

5. How does Edmund feel when he is reunited with Lucy? Edmund insincerely apologizes to Lucy about the wardrobe, and he feels very uncomfortable when Lucy tells him about the White Witch.

Quotation

… for she knew, though Edmund did not, that this was enchanted Turkish Delight and that anyone who had once tasted it would want more and more of it, and would even, if they were allowed, go on eating it till they killed themselves.

Discussion Questions

1. In terms of Christian allegory, in which one thing represents another, what do you think each of the following represents?
   - *the Queen of Narnia*
   - *Turkish Delight*
2. Matthew 26:41 says that the spirit is willing but the flesh is weak. How does this verse relate to Chapter 4?

Enrichment

Recipe for Turkish Delight (makes approx. 80 pieces)

1¾ pints water	2 lb sugar	10 oz cornstarch	1½ tbs rosewater
2 tsp lemon juice	1 tsp cream of tartar	8 oz icing sugar	red food coloring (optional)

1. Place the sugar, ½ pint water, and lemon juice in a heavy saucepan over medium heat.
2. Stir until the sugar dissolves and the mixture boils.
3. Reduce heat, simmer gently without stirring, until the mixture reaches the soft-ball stage (238 - 245°F).
4. Remove saucepan from heat.
5. In a second large heavy saucepan over medium heat, stir together 8 oz cornstarch and the cream of tartar.
6. Gradually stir in the remaining water until no lumps remain.
7. Stir constantly, until the mixture boils and forms a thick, gluey paste.
8. Slowly pour the hot sugar syrup into the cornstarch mixture, stirring constantly.
9. Reduce heat and simmer, stirring often, for about 1 hour, or until the mixture has become a pale golden color.
10. Stir in the rosewater and add food coloring (if used).
11. Pour the mixture into the prepared baking tin and spread evenly.
12. Cool to room temperature, uncovered, allow to stand overnight to set.
13. Sift the icing sugar and a little cornstarch onto a large cutting board.
14. Turn out and cut into 1" squares with an oiled knife.
15. Roll pieces in the icing sugar mixture to coat well.
16. Store in an airtight container with sheets of waxed paper, dusted with the sugar mixture, separating every layer.

1. Although Edmund's Turkish Delight tastes delicious, it is not good for Edmund. In a paragraph below, write two reasons why this statement is true. Rewrite the first sentence of these directions into a topic sentence of your own words.

____

____

____

____

Reading Notes

"Sharp's the word!" "Fast!"

Vocabulary

Write the meaning of each bold word or phrase.

1. Edmund had been feeling … **sulky** gloomy
2. regard your brother or your sister as the more **reliable** dependable; trustworthy
3. Why don't they teach **logic** the study of thinking rightly

Comprehension Questions

Answer the following in complete sentences.

1. What does Edmund do to deeply disappoint Lucy? He lies and says to Peter and Susan that he and Lucy are only pretending about Narnia.
2. How does the Professor cast doubt onto the possibility that Lucy is lying? The Professor says that it is a very serious thing to charge someone who has always been truthful before of lying.
3. Summarize the Professor's argument about time in support of Lucy's story. The Professor's logic is that another world would probably have its own kind of time, and that if Lucy is lying, she would not have come out of hiding so quickly, but would have waited to make the lie believable.
4. How do the children end up all together in the wardrobe? The children jump into the wardrobe in an effort to hide from Mrs. Macready and the visitors.

Quotation

"Logic!" said the Professor half to himself. "Why don't they teach logic at these schools? There are only three possibilities …"

"I am trying to prevent anyone saying the really foolish thing that people often say about Him: 'I'm ready to accept Jesus as a great moral teacher, but I don't accept His claim to be God.' That is the one thing we must not say. A man who was merely a man and said the sort of things Jesus said would not be a great moral teacher. He would either be a lunatic—on a level with the man who says he is a poached egg—or else he would be the Devil of Hell. You must make your choice. Either this man was, and is, the Son of God: or else a madman or something worse."

- C. S. Lewis in *Mere Christianity*

Discussion Questions

1. In the above quote from *Mere Christianity*, C. S. Lewis builds a logic statement about Christ similar to the one the Professor uses to defend Lucy. Analyze the quote and decide what the three possible ways of seeing Jesus might be.
2. What do you think about the Professor's response to the children?

Enrichment

1. Professor Digory Kirke was inspired by a real person, Professor Kirkpatrick, whom C. S. Lewis called "Kirk" or "The Great Knock." Ask a parent to read to you about him in Chapter 9 of Lewis' autobiography, *Surprised by Joy*.
2. Memorize this definition of logic: "Logic is the science of right thinking."
   Copy or write from dictation the two sentences that begin the fourth paragraph of the chapter.
   And now we come to one of the nastiest things in this story. Up to that moment Edmund had been feeling sick, and sulky, and annoyed with Lucy for being right, but he hadn't made up his mind what to do.

Reading Notes

camphor medicine derived from the camphor tree
larder pantry

Vocabulary

Write the meaning of each bold word or phrase.

1. a charge of High **Treason** betrayal of country
2. **fraternizing** with Humans. being friendly with someone

Comprehension Questions

Answer the following in complete sentences.

1. What is the first thing Peter does when he enters the woods? Peter immediately apologizes to Lucy for not having believed in her, and he asks for her forgiveness.

2. How does Edmund accidentally reveal that he has been in the woods before? Edmund suggests that the children bear left if they are to find the lamppost, thus proving that he knows the area.

3. What terrible surprise do the children come upon? When the children go to visit Mr. Tumnus, they find that his home had been vandalized and that Tumnus has been taken prisoner by the Queen.

4. What virtue does Lucy demonstrate when she learns what happened to her friend? Lucy exemplifies loyalty to her new friend when she takes responsibility for his arrest and when she pleads with the others to help her rescue him.

5. Edmund is continually skeptical and negative throughout the journey. List three of his negative comments or questions. Possible answers include:
1) Edmund criticizes the others (to himself), calling them self-satisfied prigs.
2) He calls the trip to Tumnus' a "washout," since the Faun is not at home.
3) He argues with Lucy that they cannot help Tumnus because they have not eaten.
4) He doubts the Robin as a guide, thinking they might be led into a trap.
5) He questions whether the Faun or the Queen is right (good).
6) He points out that the children have not thought about how they will get home.

Quotation

"We can't just go home, not after this. It is all on my account that the poor Faun has got into this trouble."

Discussion Question

1. Consider that there are four children who enter Narnia together. Four is a number that often signifies completeness. Can you think of other significant groups of four?

Enrichment

1. Draw a picture of the four children following the Robin. Remember to include these details: fur coats, Tumnus' ransacked cave in the background, and lots of snow-covered trees.
2. If you were to go exploring in Narnia, which of the Pevensie kids would you want to go with you? As your topic sentence, tell who that would be, and then complete your paragraph by telling why you picked that person.

Reading Notes

festoon ribbon or garland

token something that represents or is a symbol of something else

Vocabulary

Write the meaning of each bold word or phrase.

1. their **boughs** met branches of a tree
2. and **beckoned** earnestly to them gestured to someone to come
3. a sort of **modest** expression on his face. not drawing attention to your achievements
4. gave a long sigh of **contentment**. a feeling of calm or satisfaction

Comprehension Questions

Answer the following in complete sentences.

1. Who is the Beaver, to whom the Robin leads the children? He is a friend of Tumnus', and he tells the children about Aslan.

2. How does the Beaver show that he is a friend rather than a foe of the children? The Beaver offers the handkerchief Lucy had given Tumnus as his "token" or proof of friendship.

3. How do the children react when Mr. Beaver speaks of Aslan? When Mr. Beaver speaks of Aslan, Edmund feels mysterious horror; Peter feels brave and adventurous; Susan feels pleasant, like when enjoying a delicious tune or smell; Lucy feels giddy and anxious, like the feeling at the start of a holiday.

4. Compare Edmund's reaction to the conversation about Aslan to the reactions of the other children. While the others have pleasant feelings about Aslan, Edmund's reaction is negative—the talk of Aslan makes him uncomfortable. Edmund had given in to the temptations of the Queen (tasted sin as Turkish Delight), which had separated him from Aslan's goodness.

5. Why do you think he reacts in this way? He is probably feeling guilty and perhaps fearful that his action will be judged.

6. Describe the Beavers' home in detail. The Beavers' home is snug and a bit rustic. There are no pictures or books. Instead of beds, there are bunks and all sorts of things hanging from the ceiling and walls, such as onions, oilskins, hatchets, shears, spades, and fishing equipment.

Discussion Questions

1. Who do you think Aslan represents in this story? Why?
2. While the other children notice the Beavers' home on top of the dam, Edmund looks elsewhere. Is this significant? Can you think of a Bible story that relates?
3. What special characteristics do Mr. and Mrs. Beaver have?

Enrichment

1. Locate the Beavers' house on the Map of Narnia in the Appendix. Where is the Witch's castle in relation to it?
2. Copy or write from dictation the first two sentences after Mr. Beaver says, "They say Aslan is on the move—perhaps has already landed."
   And now a very curious thing happened. None of the children knew who Aslan was any more than you do; but the moment the Beaver had spoken these words everyone felt quite different.

Reading Notes

strategem plan of attack
Jinn demon

Vocabulary

Write the meaning of each bold word or phrase.

1. Because of another **prophecy** a prediction
2. the green ice of the pool had **vanished** disappeared
3. I said to myself "**Treacherous**." marked by betrayal of confidence or trust
4. she'll want to use him as a **decoy** a lure used by a hunter

Comprehension Questions

Answer the following in complete sentences.

1. How does Mr. Beaver describe Aslan? Mr. Beaver describes Aslan as the King, the Lord of the whole wood. He goes on to say that anyone who can appear before Aslan without shaking is either brave or just silly.
2. Describe the children's mixed feelings about Aslan. The children are eager to meet Aslan, but they are also a bit frightened by him.
3. What is the Witch's true ancestry? On what basis does she claim authority as a queen? The Witch is an offspring of Adam's first wife, Lilith, and giants. She has no real human blood, and she is not a Daughter of Eve (child of the human race).
4. What prophecy is the Witch concerned about? The Witch is concerned with the prophecy that when two Sons of Adam and two Daughters of Eve sit on the thrones at Cair Paravel, not only her reign but her life will end.

5. Why is the time at which Edmund left significant?
Mrs. Beaver points out that the time of Edmund's departure is important because it will affect how much he is able to tell the Witch about Aslan and the plans to meet him.

Quotation

"Wrong will be right, when Aslan comes in sight,
At the sound of his roar, sorrows will be no more,
When he bares his teeth, winter meets its death,
And when he shakes his mane, we shall have spring again."

Discussion Questions

1. Mr. Beaver says, "'Course he isn't safe. But he's good. He's the King, I tell you." Explain what he is trying to get across to the children.
2. Where do you think Edmund disappeared to? Explain.

Enrichment

1. This chapter is filled with Christian symbolism. List the references you find and explain them.
2. The Beavers tell the children that the Witch is descended from Lilith. Read about her in this quote from the book *Roar: A Christian Family Guide to the Chronicles of Narnia:* "According to Jewish legend, Lilith was Adam's first wife but refused to serve him or bear him a child. In Babylonian mythology, Lilith wandered the wilderness looking for children to hurt."
3. The children decide not to go to the Witch's castle to rescue Tumnus or Edmund. Do you think this is good or bad? Tell in a paragraph below, and give three reasons for your choice.

Reading Notes

turret small tower
lithe flexible; limber

Vocabulary

Write the meaning of each bold word or phrase.

1. where the **principal** railways would run ______ main; most important
2. **schemes** for keeping Peter in his place ______ secret plans meant to harm someone
3. And he stood there **gloating** over the stone lion ______ feeling great, often evil pleasure about someone's misfortune
4. it was **eerie** work crossing the courtyard. ______ unnerving, spooky

Comprehension Questions

Answer the following in complete sentences.

1. Who is Maugrim? He is a wolf and the captain of the Queen's secret police.
2. How does Edmund convince himself that his actions won't put his siblings in danger? Edmund tells himself that the Queen will not do anything very bad to the others, because she probably is not as cruel as her enemies make her out to be.
3. Describe Edmund's journey into the castle. Edmund travels in the cold (without his coat) and dark (because the days are short). He can hardly see, he slips often and bruises himself, and he is miserable from silence and loneliness.
4. What does Edmund find inside the Queen's castle? The first thing Edmund sees is an enormous lion in the moonlight, crouching as if to pounce.
5. What does Edmund do to betray the others? Edmund divulges the location of the others and tells of their plan to meet Aslan.

Quotation

"… human beings, all over the earth, have this curious idea that they ought to behave in a certain way, and cannot get rid of it. [Yet] … they do not behave in that way. They know the Law of Nature; they break it. These two facts are the foundation of clear thinking about ourselves and the universe we live in."

- C.S. Lewis in *Mere Christianity*

Discussion Questions

1. Why do you think Edmund feels differently toward Aslan than his siblings?
2. The author tells us that "deep down inside him [Edmund] knew the White Witch was cruel." How do you think Edmund knows? Read the quote above.
3. What do you think the author is trying to portray in detailing Edmund's dreary journey?
4. In this chapter, Edmund betrays his siblings and Aslan. Who do you think he represents in the Christian allegory?

Enrichment

1. Draw a picture of Edmund in the courtyard of the Witch's castle. Include statues of stone like the crouching lion, the giant, and the centaur.
2. Copy or write from dictation the first two lines of the paragraph following this sentence: "It was a huge arch but the great iron gates stood wide open."

   Edmund crept up to the arch and looked inside into the courtyard, and there he saw a sight that nearly made his heart stop beating. Just inside the gate, with the moonlight shining on it, stood an enormous lion crouched as if it was ready to spring.

Reading Notes

sluice-gate gate to control the flow of a channel of water

Vocabulary

Write the meaning of each bold word or phrase.

1. sounding tired and **pale** in the darkness. not colorful, bright, or lively
2. They felt very glad, but also **solemn**. deeply serious and sober
3. a **cordial** made of the juice a strong, sweetened liquor

Comprehension Questions

Answer the following in complete sentences.

1. Who is Father Christmas? He is a big and glad man who drives a sleigh with reindeer.
2. How does Mrs. Beaver reassure Susan? Mrs. Beaver proclaims that of course there is hope for the group. She contends that they can get to Aslan by taking unexpected routes and by keeping under cover.
3. Describe the route the group takes to meet Aslan, and explain the reasoning behind the decision to take it. The group travels on a path along the river bank, because the Witch will have to travel on higher ground with her sledge.
4. Where does the group stop to rest for the night? The group stops at a special hiding spot for Beavers.
5. What is a sign that the Witch is losing power? The appearance of Father Christmas indicates that the Witch is losing power, because she can no longer keep Christmas out of Narnia.
6. Detail the gifts each receives from Father Christmas. Mrs. Beaver receives a new sewing machine. Mr. Beaver's dam is mended and fitted with a new sluice-gate. Peter receives a shield and sword. Susan receives a bow with arrows and an ivory horn. Lucy receives a cordial of healing juice and a dagger. The entire group is left a tea party.

Quotation

Everyone knew him because, though you see people of his sort only in Narnia, you see pictures of them and hear them talked about even in our world—the world on this side of the wardrobe door. But when you really see them in Narnia it is rather different.

Discussion Questions

1. The Beavers have a secret hiding place that is available in times of need. Have Christians ever had hiding places like this?
2. Mr. Beaver says, "It isn't *Her*!" The author reminds us that this is bad grammar. Rewrite the sentence using correct grammar.

Enrichment

1. Look up pictures of Father Christmas in an encyclopedia or online resource, and compare and contrast them.
2. Make a colored pencil drawing of the gifts Father Christmas gave the Beavers and the children.
3. Read 1 Corinthians 12 in a New Testament. Who is like the Holy Spirit in this part of our story?
4. In the passage from which the quote above comes, Lewis talks about the difference between how people see Father Christmas in our world and how he really is in Narnia. Give two examples of how he is different, and one example of how he is similar.

____

____

____

____

____

____

____

____

Reading Notes

plum pudding rich pudding made with raisins and currants
dog fox male dog

Vocabulary

Write the meaning of each bold word or phrase.

1. He grinned in a **repulsive** manner disgusting
2. all the **gaiety** went out of their faces. high-spirits, merrymaking
3. Speak, **vermin**! disgusting animal or person
4. this **gluttony**, this waste, this self-indulgence too much eating or drinking

Comprehension Questions

Answer the following in complete sentences.

1. How does the White Witch treat Edmund when he arrives at her castle? The White Witch is terribly cruel to Edmund. She orders her wolves to kill the Beavers and Edmund's siblings. She also turns a merry party of creatures into stone.
2. List the cruel things the White Witch does that make Edmund realize that his "deep down" feeling about her is correct. She yells at him, calls him a fool, and offers him only dry bread and water.
3. Describe what is happening in Narnia as Aslan nears. Winter is fading in Narnia. The snow is melting, the sun beams down on the land, and the signs of spring are emerging everywhere.
4. How does the changing environment affect the White Witch's journey? The melting snow causes the sledge to get caught in the slushy ground, slowing the Witch's party down considerably.
5. Describe what Narnia looks like by the end of the chapter. The sky is blue with white clouds dancing overhead, the trees become fully alive with green leaves, and colorful flowers cover the ground.

Discussion Questions

1. What is the significance of the presence of Aslan corresponding with the changing landscape?
2. Have you noticed the creative liberty the author takes with capital letters? Why do you think he has chosen to do so? Does this look familiar at all?

Enrichment

1. The author mentions several different kinds of flowering plants when he describes Aslan's Spring conquering the Witch's winter. Look up these plants in an encyclopedia, dictionary, or other resource and then imagine them anew as they might look in this chapter.
2. Copy or write from dictation the rest of the paragraph after the Witch says, "Let that teach you to ask favor for spies and traitors. Drive on!"

   And Edmund for the first time in this story felt sorry for someone besides himself. It seemed so pitiful to think of those little stone figures sitting there all the silent days and all the dark nights, year after year, till the moss grew on them and at last even their faces crumbled away.

Reading Notes

kingfisher bird with rested head, long beak, and brilliant color

Alsatian British word for German shepherd dog

Vocabulary

Write the meaning of each bold word or phrase.

1. a **pavilion** pitched on one side a large tent
2. Rise up, Sir Peter Wolf's-**Bane**. person or thing causing someone's downfall

Comprehension Questions

Answer the following in complete sentences.

1. Contrast Peter, Susan, and Lucy's journey to Edmund's journey. Edmund is cold, tired, and hungry. He fears the Queen, and he experiences several cruel acts, including a beating from the Queen. Peter, Susan, and Lucy's walk seems like a "delicious dream." They walk slowly, taking in all the glorious sights and sounds of Spring.

2. Describe the scene surrounding Aslan's arrival. Aslan arrives in the center of a great processional. He is surrounded by grand creatures who play instruments, carry his standard and crown, and appear to guard him.

3. Explain how Aslan can be "good and terrible" at the same time. Aslan is a righteous king, which means he protects the innocent but he punishes the guilty.

4. Why doesn't Aslan assist Peter in the battle? Aslan refrains so that the "prince could win his spurs." Aslan lets Peter fight his own battle and earn his own victory, like a father who trains a child to be independent.

5. Describe the honor and instruction Peter receives at the end of the chapter. Peter is knighted and named Peter Wolf's-Bane. He is instructed to always clean his sword.

Quotation

"Peter did not feel very brave; indeed, he felt he was going to be sick. But that made no difference to what he had to do."

Discussion Questions

1. Now that you are more familiar with Aslan, list his Christ-like attributes.
2. What Biblical figure do you think Peter represents? Why?

Enrichment

1. Draw a picture of Peter's knighting after the battle with the wolf.
2. One of Jesus' disciples received a new name when he was tested. What was it? Look it up in Matthew 16:15-19.
3. Peter did not feel brave when he faced the wolf, but he faced it anyway. In a paragraph below, describe a time when you felt afraid.

Reading Notes

yew tree poisonous evergreen tree

cheek back talk, impertinent behavior

Vocabulary

Write the meaning of each bold word or phrase.

1. **Summon** all our people to me ______ to command someone to come
2. we will not **dispute** about them. ______ to disagree and argue
3. His life is **forfeit** to me. ______ lost to someone else
4. She has **renounced** the claim ______ given up something that was yours

Comprehension Questions

Answer the following in complete sentences.

1. Why does the Queen decide to do away with Edmund, even though Aslan has come? If she has Edmund killed, the prophecy cannot be fulfilled. She also intends to pursue the other children, even after Aslan leaves.

2. Explain the Deep Magic from the Dawn of Time. The Magic that the Emperor put into Narnia at the beginning of time gave the Witch the right to claim every traitor as hers and to punish every treachery with death. The Witch must have blood or all Narnia would be overturned and perish in fire and water.

3. How did the White Witch come to imagine herself the Queen? The Queen was the Emperor's hangman—the one who dealt his punishments.

4. What does the Queen have to have in order to prevent all Narnia from perishing in water and fire? The Queen has to have blood (death) in keeping with the Law.

5. How does Aslan protect Edmund from the fate he deserves? Aslan makes an arrangement with the Queen that causes her to renounce the claim on Edmund's life.

6. Who is the Emperor? He is the one who put the Deep Magic into Narnia.

Quotation

"You at least know the magic which the Emperor put into Narnia at the very beginning. You know that every traitor belongs to me as my lawful prey and that for every treachery I have a right to a kill."

Discussion Questions

1. What do you think the Deep Magic from before time represents?
2. Has anyone in the story reminded you of God the Father? Explain.
3. What Biblical story are you reminded of when Edmund is reunited with his siblings?

Enrichment

1. It almost seems as if the Witch is just as strong as Aslan—that they are equally matched opponents fighting it out for control of Narnia. But this is not the case. There is a similar view of the world called Dualism, which is the belief that good and evil are equal powers warring against each other. Christianity teaches, however, that Satan is under God's control; in fact, the devil was created by God! Yet, because the devil rebelled, he has been at war with God since the beginning of the world. Read the following quote from C.S. Lewis' *Mere Christianity* and look for the similarities between the war between the Witch and Aslan and the one between the devil and God:

   > "One of the things that surprised me when I first read the New Testament was that it talked so much about a Dark Power in the universe—a mighty evil spirit who was held to be the Power behind death and disease, and sin. The difference [from Dualism] is that Christianity thinks this Dark Power was created by God, and was good when he was created, and went wrong. Christianity agrees with Dualism that this universe is at war. But it does not think this is a war between independent powers. It thinks it is a civil war, a rebellion, and that we are living in a part of the universe occupied by the rebel."

2. Copy or write from dictation the first two sentences of the chapter.

   Now we must get back to Edmund. When he had been made to walk far further than he had ever known that anybody *could* walk, the Witch at last halted in a dark valley all overshadowed with fir trees and yew trees.

Reading Notes

ford shallow place in a stream or river that may be crossed

gibber to speak too quickly to be understood

Vocabulary

Write the meaning of each bold word or phrase.

1. his plan of **campaign**. a series of operations
2. the two girls **groped** their way felt about blindly
3. the Deep Magic will be **appeased**. satisfied; relieved

Comprehension Questions

Answer the following in complete sentences.

1. Where do Aslan and the children camp for the night? The group camps at the Fords of Beruna.
2. Describe the mood at camp that evening. Because Aslan seems sad and resigned, the mood at the camp is somber.
3. What happens to Aslan at the Stone Table? The Witch and her army tie Aslan, then proceeded to taunt and torture him. He is ultimately killed at the hand of the Witch.
4. How do the onlookers treat Aslan during his ordeal? The onlookers, excluding the children, try to degrade and humiliate Aslan. They shave and muzzle him, spit at, hit, and kick him.
5. What cruel intention does the White Witch share with Aslan before she kills him? The Witch admits that after she kills Aslan, she intends to kill Edmund anyway, regardless of their agreement.
6. Who are the Cruels, Hags, Incubuses, Wraiths, Horros, Efreets, Sprites, Orknies, Wooses, and Ettins? They are evil creatures on the Witch's side whom the wolf had summoned.

Quotation

"Muzzle him!" said the Witch. And even now, as they worked about his face putting on the muzzle, one bite from his jaws would have cost two or three of them their hands. But he never moved.

Discussion Questions

1. Which Biblical people, places, or events do you think the following represent? Explain.
   - Fords of Beruna
   - Susan and Lucy
   - the Stone Table
   - Aslan's capture
   - Aslan's death
2. Can you think of others?
3. In this chapter, Susan and Lucy ask to accompany Aslan during his walk. In the Bible, who asks Christ, "Quo vadis?" and gets a response similar to the one Aslan gives the girls?

Enrichment

1. Locate the Fords of Beruna and the Stone Table on the Map of Narnia in the Appendix.
2. Compare the events of Aslan's last hours with those of Jesus:
   - Aslan's "last supper" (John 13)
   - Aslan doesn't resist his enemies (John 18:7-11)
   - The girls wait and watch (Matthew 27:55-56)
3. If you were to write this chapter, how would you change it? Tell in a paragraph below.

____

____

____

____

____

____

____

____

____

Reading Notes

skirling a shrill sound like bagpipes

incantation magic spell

Vocabulary

Write the meaning of each bold word or phrase.

1. the whole of that **vile** rabble disgusting or foul
2. the ropes were all **gnawed** through. worn away by chewing
3. a **romp** as no one has ever had very lively, carefree play

Comprehension Questions

Answer the following in complete sentences.

1. List Susan and Lucy's actions at the scene of Aslan's death. Susan and Lucy go to Aslan as soon as it is safe to do so. They kneel down and kiss him, stroke his fur, remove his muzzle, and try to untie the cords that bind him.

2. Who assists the girls in untying Aslan's cords? Hundreds of little field mice nibble through the ropes until they bind Aslan no longer.

3. What do the girls find when they look toward the Stone Table at dawn? When the sun rises, the girls notice a large crack in the Stone Table, and they see that Aslan is no longer there.

4. According to the Deeper Magic that the White Witch did not know, what happens when a victim who has committed no crime is killed in a traitor's stead?
Under these circumstances, the Table will crack and death itself will start working backward.

5. Describe the girls' ride with Aslan. What do you think the author is trying to convey?
The ride with Aslan is pure joy. The girls think it is the most wonderful experience they have ever had. The author is perhaps trying to convey the happiness, security, and completeness the girls feel after being reunited with the King.

Quotation

"It means," said Aslan, "that though the Witch knew the Deep Magic, there is a magic deeper still which she did not know. Her knowledge goes back only to the dawn of time. But if she could have looked a little further back, into the stillness and the darkness before Time dawned, she would have read there a different incantation."

Discussion Questions

1. If you could think of one word to describe the Deeper Magic, what would it be?
2. The author has shown characters crying several times in the story. Children often cry when they do not get what they want, are physically hurt, or are disciplined for misbehavior. For what reasons do the children in this story cry?

Enrichment

1. Kathryn Lindskoog, an expert on C. S. Lewis, thinks that his idea of the Stone Table was probably influenced by a stone structure located in England. Do some research on historic stone structures and see if you can discover which stone structure it was.
2. Copy or write from dictation the sentence that comes right after the quote above.
She would have known that when a willing victim who had committed no treachery was killed in a traitor's stead, the Table would crack and Death itself would start working backward.

Reading Notes

saccharine tablet sugar substitute in the form of a pill

Vocabulary

Write the meaning of each bold word or phrase.

1. dazzling **plumage** of birds feathers of a bird
2. some poor prisoner may be **concealed**. hidden
3. crowd of **liberated** statues freed

Comprehension Questions

Answer the following in complete sentences.

1. What do you think is the significance of the statues coming back to life? The return of the statues to life reinforces the fact that Aslan conquered and reversed death.
2. Describe the sights and sounds of the courtyard as the statues awaken. The courtyard is a blaze of colors and ring with the happy sounds of shouts, songs, and laughter.
3. To what good use is Lucy's handkerchief? Giant Rumblebuffin uses the handkerchief to wipe the sweat from his brow after knocking down the gates and walls of the White Witch's castle.
4. Describe Aslan's army as they search out the Queen, and the battle. The chase to the Queen is like an English fox hunt, with the increasingly intense sounds of gallops, roars, and clashing metals.
5. Who is Giant Rumblebuffin? He is a nice giant of the respected Buffin family.

Quotation

"Those who are good with their noses must come in the front with us lions to smell out where the battle is." ... The most pleased of the lot was the other lion who kept running about everywhere pretending to be very busy but really in order to say to everyone he met, "Did you hear what he said? Us Lions. That means him and me. Us Lions. That's what I like about Aslan. No side, no stand-offishness. Us Lions. That meant him and me."

Discussion Questions

1. Does Giant Rumblebuffin remind you of another person or character? Explain.
2. In the quotation above, what do you think the author is trying to get across by focusing on how Aslan says "us lions"?

Enrichment

1. Draw a picture of the courtyard as the animals come back to life.
2. C. S. Lewis said in *Mere Christianity* that a person who has come from living a Natural life to a Spiritual life is like a statue that has turned into a real man. He wrote, "That is precisely what Christianity is about. This world is a great sculptor's shop. We are the statues and there is a rumor going round the shop that some of us are someday going to come to life."
3. See how long you and a friend or family member can stay in one position without moving. Choose an uncomfortable or difficult position and see who gives up first. How does it feel to be finally free to move?
4. We have met many great characters in this story, as well as this very chapter. Pick one of your favorites (besides Aslan), and give two reasons why he/she is your favorite.

Reading Notes

consorts partners, companions
score twenty or more; several

Vocabulary

Write the meaning of each bold word or phrase.

1. and **revelry** and dancing loud merrymaking
2. I never hunted a nobler **quarry**. a hunted animal; prey
3. the like **foreboding** stirreth in my heart a feeling that evil or misfortune is coming

Comprehension Questions

Answer the following in complete sentences.

1. How does Edmund turn around the battle with the Witch? Edmund wisely goes after the Witch's wand (her source of power) rather than attacking the Witch herself.
2. How does Mr. Beaver explain the quiet exit of Aslan? Mr. Beaver explains that Aslan comes and goes and doesn't like being tied down, that he has other countries to attend to, and that he will drop in when he feels like it. He is wild, not like a tame lion.
3. What nicknames do the children (Kings and Queens) acquire during their reigns? Peter is King Peter the Magnificent, Susan is Susan the Gentle, Edmund is King Edmund the Just, and Lucy is Queen Lucy the Valiant.
4. Who is the White Stag? He is a stag that will give you wishes if you catch him.
5. How do the children end up back at the Professor's house? The Kings and Queens enter the thicket, remember that what they have seen is called a lamppost, and, before they have gone twenty paces, notice that they are making their way not through branches but coats.
6. What is the Professor's reaction to the children's tale? What does he predict regarding the children's adventures? The Professor believes their whole story and does not tell them to stop being silly and telling lies. He predicts they will return to Narnia.

Discussion Questions

1. Some believe that each of the seven books in the Narnia series represents one of the seven deadly sins. Look at the list below of the sins and their descriptions. Select the sin you believe *The Lion, the Witch and the Wardrobe* focuses on, and explain why.
    - Extravagance (luxuria) - excessive luxury
    - Gluttony (gula) - excessive eating and drinking
    - Greed (avaritia) - excessive desire for something
    - Discouragement/Sloth (acedia) - laziness and apathy toward God
    - Wrath (ira) - excessive anger and hate
    - Envy (invidia) - excessive want for something belonging to another
    - Pride (superbia) - excessive sense of self-importance, superiority, or worth

Enrichment

1. Find Cair Paravel on the Map of Narnia in the Appendix.
2. C. S. Lewis was a medieval scholar, and he knew that the stag was a symbol during the Middle Ages for something very important. Can you discover what?
3. In a letter that Lewis wrote to a woman named Ann, he said that each of the Narnia books is about a truth from Christianity. Read the other Narnia books, and see if you can match the books with their main truth below

E 1. The Magician's Nephew	A. The continuing war with the powers of darkness
G 2. The Lion, The Witch and the Wardrobe	B. Restoration of the true religion after corruption
B 3. Prince Caspian	C. The spiritual life of a Christian
F 4. The Horse and His Boy	D. The Antichrist, end of the world, and Judgment
C 5. The Voyage of the Dawn Treader	E. The Creation and how evil entered the world (Narnia)
A 6. The Silver Chair	F. The calling and conversion of unbelievers
D 7. The Last Battle	G. The Crucifixion and Resurrection

4. Perhaps one of the most interesting theories about the Narnia books is that they each express and embody a planet's qualities. Read about "Planet Narnia" in the Appendix.
5. In the world of Narnia, and all worlds of the imagination, we get the chance to see life a little differently. Pick an example of something that exists in the real world but looks or acts differently in Narnia. Tell how it exists in the real world, and how it is different in Narnia.

Appendix

UNITED
KINGDOM
Scotland
N. Ireland
IRELAND
Wales
England
London

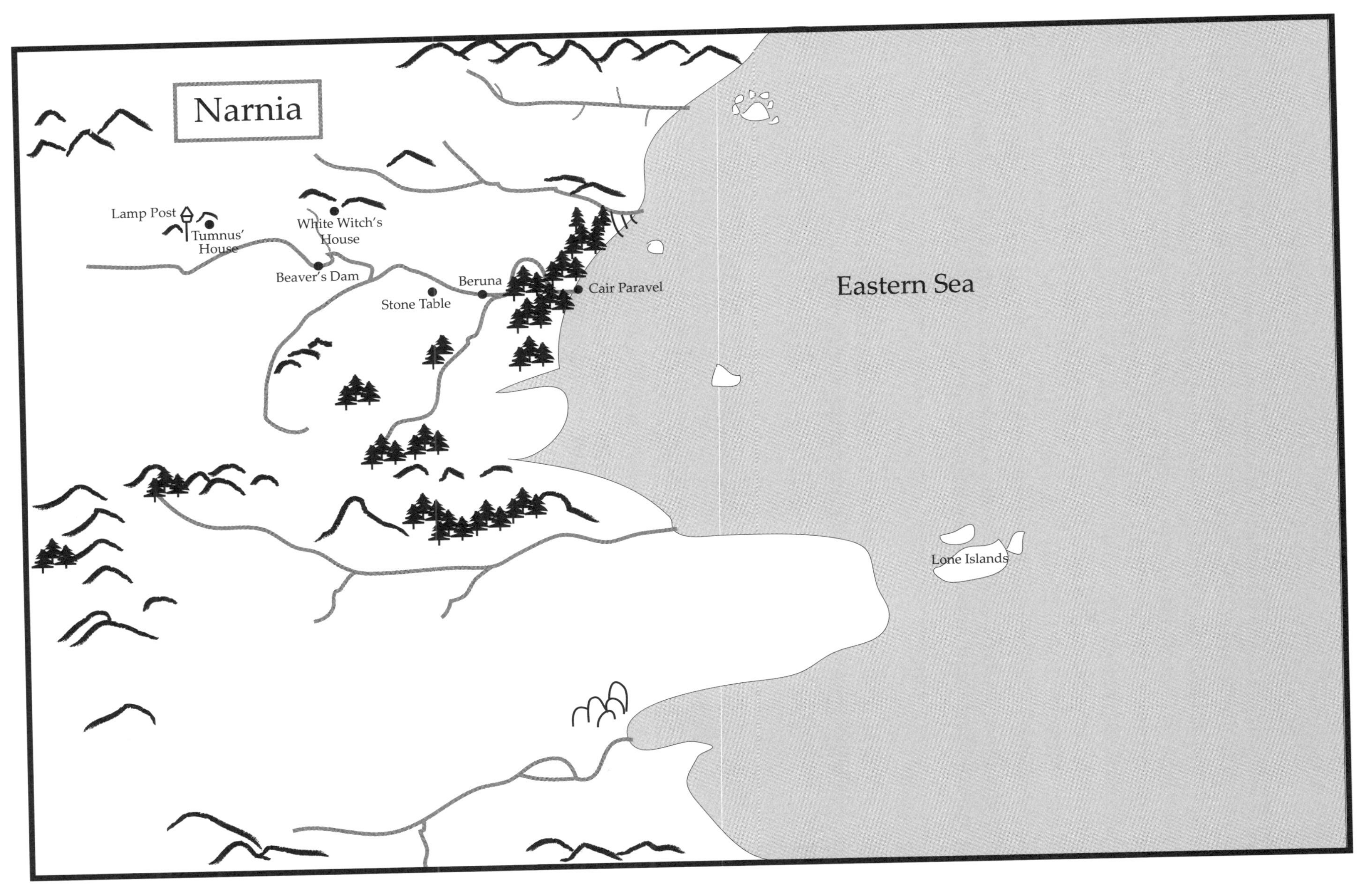
Narnia
Lamp Post
Tumnus' House
White Witch's House
Beaver's Dam
Stone Table
Beruna
Cair Paravel
Eastern Sea
Lone Islands

Planet Narnia

A C. S. Lewis expert named Michael Ward wrote a book in 2008 entitled *Planet Narnia: The Seven Heavens in the Imagination of C. S. Lewis.* In it, the author explains his theory about how *The Chronicles of Narnia* are coherent, or written with a connecting theme. The theme, Ward says, is based on the medieval understanding of the planets. People in the Middle Ages believed there were seven planets (Moon, Mercury, Venus, Sun, Mars, Jupiter, and Saturn), and each one had certain qualities particular to it. Of course, C. S. Lewis was a medieval scholar, and he knew all about this view of the heavenly bodies; in fact, he wrote an entire book about it, called *The Discarded Image*. Many of his other books deal with the planets, such as the fiction novels of his Space Trilogy. Michael Ward believes if we look carefully, we can see a relationship between the seven plants and the seven books of the *Chronicles*. Below is a brief description of each planet according to medieval thought, as well as the name of the Narnia book possibly related to it.

Luna (the Moon)

Qualities: envy; wateriness; confusion; lunacy; boundary between certainty and changeableness; sponsor of hunting and wandering

Narnia book: *The Silver Chair*

Mercury

Qualities: swiftness; heraldry; skill in speech and learning; liveliness; ability to pull apart and put back together

Narnia book: *The Horse and His Boy*

Venus

Qualities: sweetness; warmth; beauty; laughter; motherliness; fertility; vitality; creativity

Narnia book: *The Magician's Nephew*

Sol (the Sun)

Qualities: wisdom; generosity; freedom; riches; enlightenment; opposition to greed

Narnia book: *The Voyage of the Dawn Treader*

Mars

Qualities: vegetative growth in the month of March; military strength and knightly discipline; courage and orderliness, or cruelty and lawlessness

Narnia book: *Prince Caspian*

Jupiter

Qualities: kingliness; festivity and joy; tragic splendor; summer-time peacefulness

Narnia book: *The Lion, the Witch and the Wardrobe*

Saturn

Qualities: disease; betrayal; disaster; death; godly sorrow; remorse; contemplation

Narnia book: *The Last Battle*

Discussion Questions
Answer Key

Chapter 1

1. Read the second sentence of the chapter, quoted above. What can you deduce from this sentence?

    The story is set in Great Britain during World War II.

2. Compare the Faun to the satyrs and nymphs of *D'Aulaires' Book of Greek Myths*.

    With the upper body of a man and the lower body of a goat, the Faun corresponds to the satyr of *D'Aulaires' Book of Greek Myths*.

3. Discuss the significance of the lamppost.

    Light represents truth, knowledge, and goodness. Like a lighthouse, a lamppost guides lost travelers and shows the way home.

4. Can you think of other stories in which children travel to other worlds?

    Possible answers may include the following: *Alice in Wonderland, Peter Pan, Where the Wild Things Are, The Wizard of Oz*.

Chapter 2

1. Tumnus explains that it is always winter in Narnia. What feelings does winter evoke? Can you think of another story in which the seasons represent feelings?

    Winter, excluding the holidays, can be dreary, dull, joyless, and cold. The days are short and dark. People may be less sociable and less cheerful. The story of Demeter and Persephone dramatically illustrates the moods of the seasons (see the entry for Demeter and Persephone in *D'Aulaires' Book of Greek Myths*).

2. Given the allegorical nature of the book, can you detect any Christian symbolism yet?

    The children as Daughters of Eve and Sons of Adam; Christmas as the celebration of Christ's birth; the Queen as Evil in opposition to God.

3. This chapter is flooded with references from mythology. List them.

    Fauns, Silenus, Nymphs, Dryads, Bacchus

4. Why do you think Narnia's eternal winter does not include Christmas?

    The White Witch took over Narnia and turned it into a cold, dreary place. She forbade Christmas, the most joyful part of the winter. This symbolizes opposition to Christ.

Chapter 3

1. Why do you think the author always tells us about the wardrobe door when the children enter Narnia?

   The author uses the style with which the children enter the wardrobe to reveal their personalities. Lucy, for example, is cautious and thoughtful, while Edmund is hasty and foolish.

2. Lucy shows great strength and conviction in this chapter. How do her actions represent a fundamental Christian ideal?

   Lucy does not waver in her conviction that Narnia exists, even though the others do not believe it and tease her unkindly. Persevering faith like Lucy's is what is asked of all Christians.

3. What is your reaction to the Queen of Narnia? How does the author's description of her make you feel?

   Answers will vary.

Chapter 4

In terms of Christian allegory, in which one things represents another, what do you think each of the following represents?

- the Queen of Narnia = evil; opposition to Christ
- Turkish Delight = sin; temptation

4. Matthew 26:41 says that the spirit is willing but the flesh is weak. How does this verse relate to Chapter 4?

   Edmund is initially hesitant with the White Witch and is a bit afraid of her. After tasting the Turkish Delight, however, he suspends reason and emotion, and he lets his human appetites direct him.

Chapter 5

1. In the above quote from *Mere Christianity*, C. S. Lewis builds a logic statement about Christ similar to the one the Professor uses to defend Lucy. Analyze the quote and decide what the three possible ways of seeing Jesus might be.

   C.S. Lewis, in his famous argument, states that logic proves that Jesus cannot be merely a man who was a good moral teacher. Because he claimed to be the Son of God, the Savior of mankind, there are only three possible natures of Jesus:

   1. Jesus was knowingly telling falsehoods, so he was a liar who was not good or moral.
   2. Jesus was telling falsehoods but believed he was telling the truth, and so he was insane.
   3. Jesus was telling the truth, and so he was divine.

2. What do you think about the Professor's response to the children?

   Answers will vary.

Chapter 6

1. Consider that there are four children who enter Narnia together. Four is a number that often signifies completeness. Can you think of other significant groups of four?

   Four Gospels, Four Winds, Four Seasons, Four Corners of the Earth, Four Horsemen of the Apocalypse, Four Elements

Chapter 7

1. Who do you think Aslan represents in this story? Why?

   Although we do not know much about Aslan yet, we might guess that he represents goodness, opposition to evil (the Queen), authority, and safety, due to the circumstances of his "movement," the way in which the Beavers speak of him, and the way the children react to his name. When we think about who possesses all of these attributes, we might wonder if Aslan represents Christ.

2. While the other children notice the Beavers' home on top of the dam, Edmund looks elsewhere. Is this significant? Can you think of a Bible story that relates?

   Edmund is distracted by his desire to return to the Queen. He is seeking out her castle in the snow. The story of Lot's wife, who looks back toward a life of sin and becomes a pillar of salt, comes to mind.

3. What special characteristics do Mr. and Mrs. Beaver have?

   The Beavers possess the admirable qualities of self-sacrifice, courage, loyalty, faithfulness, persistence, friendship, and generosity.

Chapter 8

1. Mr. Beaver says, "'Course he isn't safe. But he's good. He's the King, I tell you." Explain what he is trying to get across to the children.

   Mr. Beaver is trying to convey to the children that Aslan is loving and fair, but that he is also powerful and just (willing to punish wrong).

2. Where do you think Edmund disappeared to? Explain.

   In the previous chapter, we noticed that Edmund was quite distracted by the Witch's castle. It is probable that he left to find the White Witch and claim the rewards she promised.

Chapter 9

1. Why do you think Edmund feels differently toward Aslan than his siblings?

   Edmund has separated himself from Aslan's goodness (grace) by giving in to temptation and sin. Rather than welcoming him eagerly, Edmund resists the judgment associated with Aslan's presence.

2. The author tells us that "deep down inside him [Edmund] knew the White Witch was cruel." How do you think Edmund knows? Read the quote above.

   As a Son of Adam (human), Edmund has an intrinsic knowledge of a natural, moral law. C. S. Lewis, in *Mere Christianity*, gives a lot of time to this inborn understanding of good and evil and the "God-sized holes" in man's heart.

3. What do you think the author was trying to portray in detailing Edmund's dreary journey?

   The author was possibly trying to portray that the road to sin is dreary and lonely.

4. In this chapter, Edmund betrays his siblings and Aslan. Who do you think he represents in the Christian Allegory?

   Edmund could be compared to Judas, who betrayed Jesus.

Chapter 10

1. The Beavers have a secret hiding place that is available in times of need. Have Christians ever had hiding places like this?

   Early Christians of Rome congregated in secret, usually in one another's private houses. There were also a few small, secret chapels. There is a persistent legend that early Christians congregated in the catacombs of Rome. The catacombs were active cemeteries in which bodies were laid out, covered only in cloth. The catacombs were dark, smelly, and unwholesome.

2. Mr. Beaver says, "It isn't *Her*!" The author reminds us that this is bad grammar. Rewrite the sentence using correct grammar.

   "It isn't *She*!"

Chapter 11

1. What is the significance of the presence of Aslan corresponding with the changing landscape?

   Aslan's presence indicates the dawn of a new era, a new world. The author uses the changing seasons in Narnia to symbolize this change and prepare the reader for the impact of Aslan.

2. Have you noticed the creative liberty the author takes with capital letters? Why do you think he has chosen to do so? Does this look familiar at all?

   The author frequently capitalizes common nouns to indicate identity (like a proper noun would). He also capitalizes pronouns when they refer to Aslan as a sign of reverence—as is done when God is referred to in the Bible and elsewhere.

Chapter 12

1. Now that you are more familiar with Aslan, list his Christ-like attributes.

   Aslan is powerful, gentle, terrifying, warm, wise, stern, and unquestioningly good, as demonstrated by several events in the book.

2. What Biblical figure do you think Peter represents? Why?

   Peter represents St. Peter (the Rock), the disciple who led the church at its beginning. Peter leads his siblings in defense of Aslan, the Christ figure in the story.

Chapter 13

1. What do you think the Deep Magic from before time represents?

   Possible answers include natural moral law, the Old Testament, and the Ten Commandments.

2. Has anyone in the story reminded you of God the Father? Explain.

   The Emperor-beyond-the-Sea may represent God the Father because he put the Deep Magic into Narnia at the Dawn of Time, which implies he is eternal. He is also Aslan's father, which is like God being the Father to His son, Jesus, whom Aslan represents in the story.

3. What Biblical story are you reminded of when Edmund is reunited with his siblings?

   The return of Edmund reminds us of the story of the Prodigal Son.

Chapter 14

1. Which Biblical people, places, or events do you think the following represent? Explain.

   Fords of Beruna - Garden of Gethsemane

   Susan and Lucy - Mary, mother of Jesus, and Mary Magdalene

   the Stone Table - Calvary or Golgotha

   Aslan's capture - the capture of Jesus

   Aslan's death - the Crucifixion

2. Can you think of others?

   Answers will vary.

3. In this chapter, Susan and Lucy ask to accompany Aslan during his walk. In the Bible, who asks Christ, "Quo vadis?" and gets a response similar to the one Aslan gives the girls?

   In John 13:36, Jesus told the Apostles that he would only be with them a bit longer. Peter asked, "Quo vadis, Domine?" ("Where are you going, Lord?") Jesus answered, "Where I am going you cannot follow now, but you will follow later."

Chapter 15

1. If you could think of one word to describe the Deeper Magic, what would it be?

   Answers may include: grace, substitution, atonement, salvation.

2. The author has shown characters crying several times in the story. Children often cry when they do not get what they want, are physically hurt, or are disciplined for misbehavior. For what reasons do the children in this story cry?

   They cry for good reasons, such as feeling deep grief over the loss (i.e., Lucy and Susan for Aslan) or near loss (i.e., Peter and Susan after the wolf's attack) of someone they love, or feeling a sense of injustice and distrust put upon them (i.e., Lucy when her siblings disbelieve her story).

Chapter 16

1. Does Giant Rumblebuffin remind you of another person or character? Explain.

   It is apparent that the author is quite familiar with Greek mythology, given the abundant references throughout the book. The Giant is somewhat reminiscent of Hephaestus.

2. In the quotation above, what do you think the author is trying to get across by focusing on how Aslan says "us lions"?

   Aslan's important use of the pronoun "us" is probably intended to convey the significance and magnitude of God becoming man, like us, through Christ, to show His love for us, to bear our burdens and guilt, and to give us an example to imitate.

Chapter 17

1. Some believe that each of the seven books in the Narnia series represents one of the seven deadly sins. Look at the list below of the sins and their descriptions. Select the sin you believe *The Lion, the Witch and the Wardrobe* focuses on, and explain why.

   Answers will vary. (Don King argues gluttony is demonstrated by Edmund in *The Lion, the Witch and the Wardrobe*.)

Quizzes & Final Test

(reproducible for classroom use)

LWW Quiz I

Chapters 1-4

Name ______________________________

Date ______________________________

Vocabulary Matching: Write the letter of the vocabulary word on the line. (10 points)

1. _______ queer
2. _______ parcel
3. _______ hoax
4. _______ jeered
5. _______ flushed

a. something wrapped up in paper; a package
b. a trick to make something seem real
c. laughed scornfully at someone
d. strange
e. red in the face; rose-cheeked

Vocabulary Usage: Fill in the blank with the appropriate vocabulary word. (10 points)

dominions	**enchanted**	**geography**	**innocent**	**inquisitive**
kettle	**ordinary**	**stern**		

1. The sound of the steaming ____________________ woke the sleepy man from his nap.
2. Jill was taught a lesson in ____________________ about the British Ilses.
3. It seemed like another ____________________ day, but then a strange thing happened.
4. An ____________________ person will not run from the police, but a guilty man will.
5. A ____________________ look from his father stopped the boy from his mischief.

Multiple Choice: Circle the best answer for each question. (10 points)

1. The author of *The Lion, the Witch and the Wardrobe* is:
   a. J. R. R. Tolkien
   b. C. S. Lewis
   c. Eric Knight
   d. Laura Ingalls Wilder
2. The four children are:
   a. Peter, Susan, Edward, Lucy
   b. Peter, Sarah, Edward, Lucy
   c. Peter, Susan, Edmund, Lucy
   d. Peter, Sarah, Edmund, Lucy

3. The place to which the children go to live is:
   a. a large house in the country owned by a professor
   b. a boarding school run by a priest
   c. a house in London owned by their father
   d. a castle in the country where their grandfather lives
4. Tumnus is:
   a. a dwarf in service of the Queen
   b. a naiad Lucy meets in the woods
   c. a faun who lives in Narnia
   d. a guide who helps Edmund find the wardrobe
5. The Queen is:
   a. the monarch who rules England
   b. Tumnus' master
   c. the good witch who has always ruled Narnia
   d. a tall, pale, proud witch dressed in white

Comprehension Short Answer: Answer each question or fill in the blanks. (10 points)

1. When ______________________ first travels through the wardrobe, she discovers two rows of fur coats and then a snow-covered wood at nighttime.
2. What does Tumnus confess to Lucy? ____
   ____
3. Lucy is miserable for several days following her adventure because ______________________
   ____
4. The effect the ______________________ has on Edmund is that he gets hooked on it.
5. What does the Queen promise to give Edmund if he does what she asks him? ______________
   ____

Composition: Write from dictation the paragraph in Chapter 3 that begins after, "It was a beautiful face in other respects, but proud and cold and stern." (10 points)

____
____
____
____
____

Rubric and Points Possible:
Capitalization __/ 2 pts.; Punctuation __/ 2 pts.; Correct words __/ 6 pts.

LWW Quiz 2

Chapters 5-9

Name ______________________

Date ______________________

Vocabulary Matching: Write the letter of the vocabulary word on the line. (10 points)

1. ______ fraternizing
2. ______ principal
3. ______ reliable
4. ______ sulky
5. ______ gloating

a. gloomy, withdrawn, sullen
b. dependable; trustworthy
c. associating in a friendly way
d. main; most important
e. feeling great, often evil, pleasure about someone's misfortune

Vocabulary Usage: Fill in the blank with the appropriate vocabulary word. (10 points)

beckoned	**bough**	**contentment**	**decoy**	**eerie**
logic	**modest**	**prophecy**	**treacherous**	**schemes**
treason	**vanished**			

1. The hunter used a ______________________ to lure the animal into his trap.
2. An __________ sound echoed in the valley and unnerved even the bravest soldier.
3. A wicked person's ______________________ against an innocent person will backfire.
4. The woman in line at the restaurant was ____________________ by the hostess to follow.
5. Five girls sat chatting on the large ______________________ of the tree.

Multiple Choice: Circle the best answer for each question. (10 points)

1. Mr. Beaver is:

   a. a red-breasted robin who guides the children
   b. a friend of Tumnus' who tells them about Aslan
   c. a beaver who secretly works for the White Witch
   d. the real name of the Professor

2. Mrs. Beaver is:

   a. the name the children give to Mrs. Macready
   b. Mr. Beaver's accomplice and servant to the Queen
   c. Mr. Beaver's kind wife
   d. Mr. Beaver's wife who helps the children escape from him

3. The Beavers' home is:
   a. a large house in the country
   b. a comfortable and cozy cave next door to Mr. Tumnus
   c. the dark woods where some trees serve the Witch
   d. a snug and rustic home on the beavers' dam
4. Mr. Beaver describes Aslan as:
   a. the prince of Narnia who lives over the Sea
   b. the King of Narnia and the Lord of the whole wood
   c. a lion turned to stone in the Witch's castle
   d. the first king of Narnia before the Witch took over
5. Maugrim is:
   a. the dog who ransacked Tumnus' home
   b. the name of the Witch's castle
   c. the captain of the Queen's secret police
   d. a dwarf who guards the Witch's prisoners

Comprehension Short Answer: Answer each question or fill in the blanks. (10 points)

1. Edmund deeply disappoints Lucy by ____ ____.
2. Lucy demonstrates the virtue of ____________ to her new friend, Tumnus, by taking responsibility for his arrest and pleading for the others to help rescue him.
3. When the Beaver speaks of ____________ Peter feels brave, Susan feels pleasant, Edmund feels horror, and Lucy feels giddy.
4. The Witch is concerned about the prophecy of the two Sons of Adam and two Daughters of Eve on the thrones and the end of ______________________________.
5. Edmund betrays the others by telling the Witch ______________________________ ____.

Composition: How does Edmund convince himself that his actions won't put his siblings in danger? (10 points)

____

____

____

____

____

Rubric and Points Possible:
Answer __/ 4 pts.; Capitalization __/ 2 pts.; Punctuation __/ 2 pts.; Complete sentences __/ 2 pts.

LWW Quiz 3

Chapters 10-13

Name __________________________________

Date __________________________________

Vocabulary Matching: Write the letter of the vocabulary word on the line. (10 points)

1. _______ vermin
2. _______ bane
3. _______ gluttony
4. _______ cordial
5. _______ forfeit

a. lost to someone else
b. a strong, sweetened liquor
c. disgusting animal or person
d. person or thing causing someone's downfall
e. too much eating or drinking

Vocabulary Usage: Fill in the blank with the appropriate vocabulary word. (10 points)

dispute	**gaiety**	**pale**	**pavilion**	**renounced**
repulsive	**solemn**	**summoned**		

1. The flies swarming near his food were __________________________ pests.
2. Tired and sweaty from the long desert march, the travelers were glad to pitch the ____________________________ and rest under its shade.
3. The mistress of the boarding school ____________________________ the new girl to her office.
4. Do not _______________________with the umpire. He will only throw you out of the game.
5. All the blood left his face and he was as ___________ as a sheet of paper.

Multiple Choice: Circle the best answer for each question. (10 points)

1. Father Christmas is:
   a. just fun and jolly Santa Claus
   b. never allowed in Narnia
   c. serious and gloomy
   d. big and glad
2. The gifts the children receive are:
   a. shield, sword, bow with arrows, horn, cordial, dagger
   b. spear, battle axe, bow with arrows, horses to ride on
   c. train set, new dress, teddy bear, and candy
   d. new sewing machine, fishing pole, sluice-gate

3. Because Aslan comes nearer, Narnia is:
    a. being strewn with festoons and Christmas decorations
    b. losing its Winter and changing to Spring
    c. in great danger
    d. without any more problems
4. Aslan arrives with:
    a. no fanfare or celebration
    b. Father Christmas
    c. a great processional of creatures
    d. the Emperor beyond the Sea
5. The Emperor is:
    a. a great ruler who lives south of Narnia
    b. Aslan's brother in another world like Narnia
    c. the one whom the Witch defeated to get Narnia
    d. the one who put the Deep Magic into Narnia

Comprehension Short Answer: Answer each question or fill in the blanks. (10 points)

1. The sign that the Witch is losing her power is the appearance of ______________.
2. The changing environment affects the Witch's journey by ______________
______________.
3. Peter, Susan, and Lucy's journey is different from Edmund's because______________
______________.
4. The ______________ from the Dawn of Time gave the Witch the right to claim traitors and punish them with death, or else all Narnia will perish.
5. The Witch came to imagine herself as Queen because ______________
______________.

Composition: Write from dictation the first two sentences of Chapter 13. (10 points)

____
____
____
____
____
____

Rubric and Points Possible:
Capitalization __/ 2 pts.; Punctuation __/ 2 pts.; Correct words__/ 6 pts.

LWW Quiz 4

Chapters 14-17

Name ______________________________

Date ______________________________

Vocabulary Matching: Write the letter of the vocabulary word on the line. (10 points)

1. _______ liberated
2. _______ vile
3. _______ appeased
4. _______ revelry
5. _______ plumage

a. satisfied; relieved
b. disgusting
c. freed
d. feathers of a bird
e. loud merrymaking

Vocabulary Usage: Fill in the blank with the appropriate vocabulary word. (10 points)

gnawed	**concealed**	**foreboding**	**groped**	**vile**
campaign	**romp**	**quarry**		

1. The restless old man got up from bed and ____________________ his way through the dark to the kitchen for a midnight snack.
2. A chunk of tough bread was the only food left, and so he ____________________ on it until he realized he had forgotten to put in his false teeth.
3. Then a feeling of ____________________ came over him, and he seemed to think he was being watched.
4. He looked around to see a pair of shining red eyes in the kitchen corner, but the rest of the watcher's body was ____________________ by the dark.
5. The man quickly turned on the lights and found not an evil or ____________________ creature, but only a mouse, with a pair of false teeth in its mouth.

Multiple Choice: Circle the best answer for each question. (10 points)

1. Cruels, Hags, Incubuses, Wraiths, Horrors, Efreets, Sprites, Orknies, Wooses, and Ettins are:
   a. creatures who come to fight for Aslan
   b. evil creatures on the Witch's side whom the Wolf had summoned
   c. the creatures turned to stone in the Witch's castle
   d. none of the above
2. The little field mice are:
   a. servants of the Queen left behind to guard the Stone Table
   b. servants of Aslan who cry with Susan and Lucy
   c. the ones who untie Aslan's cord by nibbling them
   d. transformed out of stone

3. Giant Rumblebuffin is:
   a. one of the Ettins fighting for the Queen
   b. the guardian of the Witch's castle
   c. a very intelligent advisor to Aslan
   d. a nice giant of the respected Buffin family
4. The nicknames Peter, Susan, Edmund, and Lucy get as kings and queens are:
   a. Peter the Magnificent, Susan the Gentle, Edmund the Just, and Lucy the Valiant
   b. Peter the Brave, Susan the Beautiful, Edmund the Wise, and Lucy the True
   c. Peter the First, Susan the Elder, Edmund the Shrewd, and Lucy the Sweet
   d. Peter the Brave, Susan the Beautiful, Edmund the Just, and Lucy the Valiant
5. The White Stag is:
   a. a royal messenger for the kings and queens of Narnia
   b. a guide to other worlds
   c. a stag that would give you wishes if you caught him
   d. a sign that Aslan has returned

Comprehension Short Answer: Answer each question or fill in the blanks. (10 points)

1. At the ________________________, Aslan is tied, taunted, tortured, and killed.
2. According to the Deeper Magic, killing Aslan would ____________________________________

   ____.
3. The ride with Aslan is the most wonderful experience _______________ and _______________

   have ever had.
4. The significance of the statues coming to life is that it ____________________________

   ____.
5. Mr. Beaver explains that Aslan left quietly because ________________________________

   ____.

Composition: What is the Professor's reaction to the children's tale? What does he predict regarding the children's adventures? (10 points)

____

____

____

____

Rubric and Points Possible:
Answer __/ 4 pts.; Capitalization __/ 2 pts.; Punctuation __/ 2 pts.; Complete sentences __/ 2 pts.

LWW Final Exam

Name ______________________________

Date ______________________________

Vocabulary Matching: Write the letter of the vocabulary word on the line. (10 points)

1. _______ campaign
2. _______ quarry
3. _______ solemn
4. _______ gaiety
5. _______ renounced
6. _______ modest
7. _______ contentment
8. _______ treason
9. _______ enchanted
10. _______ inquisitive

a. deeply serious and sober
b. high-spirits, merrymaking
c. a feeling of calm or satisfaction
d. a hunted animal; prey
e. curious, or wanting to know more
f. put under a spell
g. a series of operations
h. not drawing attention to your achievements
i. betrayal of country
j. given up something that was yours

Vocabulary Usage: Fill in the blank with the appropriate vocabulary word. (10 points)

appeased	**bane**	**flushed**	**forfeit**	**fraternizing**
gloating	**hoax**	**jeered**	**liberated**	**principal**
reliable	**vermin**			

1. In old times sailors used the North Star for navigating their ships, because it is the most ______________________________, or dependable, guidepost in the sky.
2. Odysseus was trapped on the island of Calypso, but he was ______________________________ when Hermes convinced her to let him go free.
3. The god Poseidon wrecked Odysseus' boat, and Odysseus had to ______________________________ his clothes so that he could swim more easily to the shore.
4. The giant Cyclops was the ______________________ of many of Odysseus' men, whom he ate.
5. Odysseus was able to blind the giant, but instead of ______________________________ over the giant and foolishly revealing who he was, he should have immediately run away.
6. When he finally arrived home, he was ____________________________ at by young men because he looked old and poor, and they did not know he was Odysseus.
7. Odyssesus was playing a ________________________ on the men, and he waited to reveal himself at just the right time.

8. Finally, Odysseus took off his disguise and ______________________ his anger at the young men, who had tried to steal his wife and possessions.

9. Odysseus killed all his enemies, including anyone he had seen ______________________ with the young men.

10. His wife did not believe he was Odysseus at first, and his face ______________________ with hurt and anger. In the end, however, she believed him.

Multiple Choice: Circle the best answer for each question. (10 points)

1. The author of *The Lion, the Witch and the Wardrobe* is:
   a. Jr. Tolkien
   b. J. R. R. Tolkien
   c. C. R. Lewis
   d. C. S. Lewis

2. The place to which the children go to live is:
   a. a boarding school run by Digory Kirke
   b. a house in London after the war
   c. a large house in the country owned by a professor
   d. a castle in the north country of England

3. The Beavers' home is:
   a. a large house in the Wild Wood
   b. a comfortable and cozy cave next door to Tumnus
   c. a snug and rustic home on the beavers' dam
   d. a cottage near the Fords of Beruna

4. Mr. Beaver describes Aslan as:
   a. a fierce and wild warrior
   b. the prince of Narnia from over the Sea
   c. the first king of Narnia before the Witch
   d. the King of Narnia and the Lord of the whole wood

5. The gifts the children receive are:
   a. a spear, battle axe, bow with arrows, horses to ride on
   b. shield, sword, horn, cordial, and dagger
   c. tea party, sewing machine, fishing gear, sluice-gate
   d. shield, sword, bow with arrows, horn, cordial, dagger

6. Because Aslan comes nearer, Narnia is:
   a. in grave peril of fire and water
   b. free from the Witch forever
   c. being decorated with festoons and banners
   d. losing its Winter and changing to Spring

7. Aslan arrives with:
    a. a great processional of creatures
    b. Father Christmas
    c. no fanfare or celebration since he is humble
    d. the Emperor Beyond the Sea
8. The Emperor is:
    a. Aslan's brother in another world like Narnia
    b. the one who put the Deep Magic into Narnia
    c. the one who made the Witch queen and protector of Narnia
    d. a great ruler who lives in the land of Calormen
9. The nicknames Peter, Susan, Edmund, and Lucy get as kings and queens are:
    a. Peter the Brave, Susan the Beautiful, Edmund the Wise, and Lucy the True
    b. Peter the Magnificent, Susan the Beautiful, Edmund the Just, and Lucy the True
    c. Peter the Magnificent, Susan the Gentle, Edmund the Just, and Lucy the Valiant
    d. Peter the Brave, Susan the Gentle, Edmund the Wise, and Lucy the Valiant
10. The White Stag is:
    a. a stag that would give you wishes if you caught him
    b. a guide to other worlds
    c. a sign of Aslan's return
    d. a royal messenger for the kings and queens of Narnia

Comprehension Short Answer: Answer each question or fill in the blanks. (10 points)

1. Lucy is miserable for several days following her adventure because ______________________________ ____.
2. The effect the Turkish Delight has on Edmund is ______________________________.
3. When the Beaver speaks of Aslan, Peter feels ____________________, Susan feels ____________ ____________, Edmund feels ______________, and Lucy feels ______________.
4. Edmund betrays the others by ____ ____.
5. The sign that the Witch is losing her power is ______________________________________ ____.
6. The Deep Magic from the Dawn of Time gave the Witch the right to claim traitors and punish them with ________________________, or else all Narnia will ____________________.
7. The Witch came to imagine herself as Queen because she was the Emperor's ______________.
8. According to the ____________________________, when a victim who has committed no crime is killed in a traitor's stead, the Table will crack and death will start working backwards.

9. The significance of the statues coming to life is ____
____.

10. Mr. Beaver explains that Aslan left quietly because he is not a ______________________________.

Composition: (10 points each)

1. Write from dictation the paragraph in Chapter 3 that begins after, "It was a beautiful face in other respects, but proud and cold and stern."

____

____

____

____

____

____

____

Rubric and Points Possible:
Capitalization __/ 2 pts.; Punctuation __/ 2 pts.; Correct words __/ 6 pts.

2. Compare Edmund's reaction to the Beaver's conversation about Aslan to the reaction of the other children. Why do you think he reacts in this way?

____

____

____

____

____

____

____

Rubric and Points Possible:
Answer __/ 4 pts.; Capitalization __/ 2 pts.; Punctuation __/ 2 pts.; Complete sentences __/ 2 pts.

LWW Quiz 1 Answer Key

Chapters 1-4

Name ______________________

Date ______________________

Vocabulary Matching: Write the letter of the vocabulary word on the line. (10 points)

1. __D__ queer
2. __A__ parcel
3. __B__ hoax
4. __C__ jeered
5. __E__ flushed

a. something wrapped up in paper; a package
b. a trick to make something seem real
c. laughed scornfully at someone
d. strange
e. red in the face; rose-cheeked

Vocabulary Usage: Fill in the blank with the appropriate vocabulary word. (10 points)

dominions	**enchanted**	**geography**	**innocent**	**inquisitive**
kettle	**ordinary**	**stern**		

1. The sound of the steaming ____kettle____ woke the sleepy man from his nap.
2. Jill was taught a lesson in ____geography____ about the British Ilses.
3. It seemed like another ____ordinary____ day, but then a strange thing happened.
4. An ____innocent____ person will not run from the police, but a guilty man will.
5. A ____stern____ look from his father stopped the boy from his mischief.

Multiple Choice: Circle the best answer for each question. (10 points)

1. The author of *The Lion, the Witch and the Wardrobe* is:
   - a. J. R. R. Tolkien
   - (b.) C. S. Lewis
   - c. Eric Knight
   - d. Laura Ingalls Wilder
2. The four children are:
   - a. Peter, Susan, Edward, Lucy
   - b. Peter, Sarah, Edward, Lucy
   - (c.) Peter, Susan, Edmund, Lucy
   - d. Peter, Sarah, Edmund, Lucy

3. The place to which the children go to live is:
   - (a.) a large house in the country owned by a professor
   - b. a boarding school run by a priest
   - c. a house in London owned by their father
   - d. a castle in the country where their grandfather lives

4. Tumnus is:
   - a. a dwarf in service of the Queen
   - b. a naiad Lucy meets in the woods
   - (c.) a faun who lives in Narnia
   - d. a guide who helps Edmund find the wardrobe

5. The Queen is:
   - a. the monarch who rules England
   - b. Tumnus' master
   - c. the good witch who has always ruled Narnia
   - (d.) a tall, pale, proud witch dressed in white

Comprehension Short Answer: Answer each question or fill in the blanks. (10 points)

1. When ___Lucy___ first travels through the wardrobe, she discovers two rows of fur coats and then a snow-covered wood at nighttime.
2. What does Tumnus confess to Lucy? ___He confesses he is a kidnapper for the White Witch.___
3. Lucy is miserable for several days following her adventure because ___Her siblings think she is telling a silly lie___
4. The effect the ___Turkish Delight___ has on Edmund is that he gets hooked on it.
5. What does the Queen promise to give Edmund if he does what she asks him? ___She promises to make him a Prince.___

Composition: Write from dictation the paragraph in Chapter 3 that begins after, "It was a beautiful face in other respects, but proud and cold and stern." (10 points)

The sledge was a fine sight as it came sweeping toward Edmund with the bells jingling and the dwarf cracking his whip and the snow flying up on each side of it.

Rubric and Points Possible:
Capitalization __/ 2 pts.; Punctuation __/ 2 pts.; Correct words __/ 6 pts.

LWW Quiz 2 Answer Key

Chapters 5-9

Name ______________________________

Date ______________________________

Vocabulary Matching: Write the letter of the vocabulary word on the line. (10 points)

1. ___C___ fraternizing
2. ___D___ principal
3. ___B___ reliable
4. ___A___ sulky
5. ___E___ gloating

a. gloomy, withdrawn, sullen
b. dependable; trustworthy
c. associating in a friendly way
d. main; most important
e. feeling great, often evil, pleasure about someone's misfortune

Vocabulary Usage: Fill in the blank with the appropriate vocabulary word. (10 points)

beckoned	**bough**	**contentment**	**decoy**	**eerie**
logic	**modest**	**prophecy**	**treacherous**	**schemes**
treason	**vanished**			

1. The hunter used a ___decoy___ to lure the animal into his trap.
2. An ___eerie___ sound echoed in the valley and unnerved even the bravest soldier.
3. A wicked person's ___schemes or treason___ against an innocent person will backfire.
4. The woman in line at the restaurant was ___beckoned___ by the hostess to follow.
5. Five girls sat chatting on the large ___bough___ of the tree.

Multiple Choice: Circle the best answer for each question. (10 points)

1. Mr. Beaver is:
   a. a red-breasted robin who guides the children
   (b.) a friend of Tumnus' who tells them about Aslan
   c. a beaver who secretly works for the White Witch
   d. the real name of the Professor
2. Mrs. Beaver is:
   a. the name the children give to Mrs. Macready
   b. Mr. Beaver's accomplice and servant to the Queen
   (c.) Mr. Beaver's kind wife
   d. Mr. Beaver's wife who helps the children escape from him

3. The Beavers' home is:
   a. a large house in the country
   b. a comfortable and cozy cave next door to Mr. Tumnus
   c. the dark woods where some trees serve the Witch
   (d.) a snug and rustic home on the beavers' dam
4. Mr. Beaver describes Aslan as:
   a. the prince of Narnia who lives over the Sea
   (b.) the King of Narnia and the Lord of the whole wood
   c. a lion turned to stone in the Witch's castle
   d. the first king of Narnia before the Witch took over
5. Maugrim is:
   a. the dog who ransacked Tumnus' home
   b. the name of the Witch's castle
   (c.) the captain of the Queen's secret police
   d. a dwarf who guards the Witch's prisoners

Comprehension Short Answer: Answer each question or fill in the blanks. (10 points)

1. Edmund deeply disappoints Lucy by lying and saying that he and Lucy are pretending about Narnia.
2. Lucy demonstrates the virtue of loyalty to her new friend, Tumnus, by taking responsibility for his arrest and pleading for the others to help rescue him.
3. When the Beaver speaks of Aslan Peter feels brave, Susan feels pleasant, Edmund feels horror, and Lucy feels giddy.
4. The Witch is concerned about the prophecy of the two Sons of Adam and two Daughters of Eve on the thrones and the end of her life and reign.
5. Edmund betrays the others by telling the Witch the location of the others and their plan to meet Aslan.

Composition: How does Edmund convince himself that his actions won't put his siblings in danger? (10 points)

Edmund tells himself that the Queen will not do anything very bad to the others, because she probably is not as cruel as her enemies make her out to be.

Rubric and Points Possible:
Answer __/ 4 pts.; Capitalization __/ 2 pts.; Punctuation __/ 2 pts.; Complete sentences __/ 2 pts.

LWW Quiz 3 Answer Key

Chapters 10-13

Name ______________________

Date ______________________

Vocabulary Matching: Write the letter of the vocabulary word on the line. (10 points)

1. C vermin
2. D bane
3. E gluttony
4. B cordial
5. A forfeit

a. lost to someone else
b. a strong, sweetened liquor
c. disgusting animal or person
d. person or thing causing someone's downfall
e. too much eating or drinking

Vocabulary Usage: Fill in the blank with the appropriate vocabulary word. (10 points)

dispute	gaiety	pale	pavilion	renounced
repulsive	solemn	summoned		

1. The flies swarming near his food were repulsive pests.
2. Tired and sweaty from the long desert march, the travelers were glad to pitch the pavilion and rest under its shade.
3. The mistress of the boarding school summoned the new girl to her office.
4. Do not dispute with the umpire. He will only throw you out of the game.
5. All the blood left his face and he was as pale as a sheet of paper.

Multiple Choice: Circle the best answer for each question. (10 points)

1. Father Christmas is:
   a. just fun and jolly Santa Claus
   b. never allowed in Narnia
   c. serious and gloomy
   (d.) big and glad
2. The gifts the children receive are:
   (a.) shield, sword, bow with arrows, horn, cordial, dagger
   b. spear, battle axe, bow with arrows, horses to ride on
   c. train set, new dress, teddy bear, and candy
   d. new sewing machine, fishing pole, sluice-gate

3. Because Aslan comes nearer, Narnia is:
   a. being strewn with festoons and Christmas decorations
   (b.) losing its Winter and changing to Spring
   c. in great danger
   d. without any more problems
4. Aslan arrives with:
   a. no fanfare or celebration
   b. Father Christmas
   (c.) a great processional of creatures
   d. the Emperor beyond the Sea
5. The Emperor is:
   a. a great ruler who lives south of Narnia
   b. Aslan's brother in another world like Narnia
   c. the one whom the Witch defeated to get Narnia
   (d.) the one who put the Deep Magic into Narnia

Comprehension Short Answer: Answer each question or fill in the blanks. (10 points)

1. The sign that the Witch is losing her power is the appearance of Father Christmas.
2. The changing environment affects the Witch's journey by slowing her down because the melting now causes her sledge to get caught on the slushy ground.
3. Peter, Susan, and Lucy's journey is different from Edmund's because they are able to enjoy their journey and Edmund's is miserable.
4. The Deep Magic from the Dawn of Time gave the Witch the right to claim traitors and punish them with death, or else all Narnia will perish.
5. The Witch came to imagine herself as Queen because she was the Emperor's hangman.

Composition: Write from dictation the first two sentences of Chapter 13. (10 points)

Now we must get back to Edmund. When he had been made to walk further than he had ever known that anybody could walk, the Witch at last halted in a dark valley all overshadowed with fir trees and yew trees.

Rubric and Points Possible:
Capitalization __/ 2 pts.; Punctuation __/ 2 pts.; Correct words__/ 6 pts.

LWW Quiz 4 Answer Key

Chapters 14-17

Name ______________________________

Date ______________________________

Vocabulary Matching: Write the letter of the vocabulary word on the line. (10 points)

1. c liberated
2. b vile
3. a appeased
4. e revelry
5. d plumage

a. satisfied; relieved
b. disgusting
c. freed
d. feathers of a bird
e. loud merrymaking

Vocabulary Usage: Fill in the blank with the appropriate vocabulary word. (10 points)

gnawed	**concealed**	**foreboding**	**groped**	**vile**
campaign	**romp**	**quarry**		

1. The restless old man got up from bed and groped his way through the dark to the kitchen for a midnight snack.
2. A chunk of tough bread was the only food left, and so he gnawed on it until he realized he had forgotten to put in his false teeth.
3. Then a feeling of foreboding came over him, and he seemed to think he was being watched.
4. He looked around to see a pair of shining red eyes in the kitchen corner, but the rest of the watcher's body was concealed by the dark.
5. The man quickly turned on the lights and found not an evil or vile creature, but only a mouse, with a pair of false teeth in its mouth.

Multiple Choice: Circle the best answer for each question. (10 points)

1. Cruels, Hags, Incubuses, Wraiths, Horrors, Efreets, Sprites, Orknies, Wooses, and Ettins are:
   a. creatures who come to fight for Aslan
   (b.) evil creatures on the Witch's side whom the Wolf had summoned
   c. the creatures turned to stone in the Witch's castle
   d. none of the above
2. The little field mice are:
   a. servants of the Queen left behind to guard the Stone Table
   b. servants of Aslan who cry with Susan and Lucy
   (c.) the ones who untie Aslan's cord by nibbling them
   d. transformed out of stone

3. Giant Rumblebuffin is:
   a. one of the Ettins fighting for the Queen
   b. the guardian of the Witch's castle
   c. a very intelligent advisor to Aslan
   (d.) a nice giant of the respected Buffin family
4. The nicknames Peter, Susan, Edmund, and Lucy get as kings and queens are:
   (a.) Peter the Magnificent, Susan the Gentle, Edmund the Just, and Lucy the Valiant
   b. Peter the Brave, Susan the Beautiful, Edmund the Wise, and Lucy the True
   c. Peter the First, Susan the Elder, Edmund the Shrewd, and Lucy the Sweet
   d. Peter the Brave, Susan the Beautiful, Edmund the Just, and Lucy the Valiant
5. The White Stag is:
   a. a royal messenger for the kings and queens of Narnia
   b. a guide to other worlds
   (c.) a stag that would give you wishes if you caught him
   d. a sign that Aslan has returned

Comprehension Short Answer: Answer each question or fill in the blanks. (10 points)

1. At the ___Stone Table___, Aslan is tied, taunted, tortured, and killed.
2. According to the Deeper Magic, killing Aslan would ___crack the Stone Table and death would start working backwards___.
3. The ride with Aslan is the most wonderful experience ___Susan___ and ___Lucy___ have ever had.
4. The significance of the statues coming to life is that it ___reinforces the fact that Aslan conquered and reversed death___.
5. Mr. Beaver explains that Aslan left quietly because ___he doesn't like being tied down / has other countries to attend to / is wild___.

Composition: What is the Professor's reaction to the children's tale? What does he predict regarding the children's adventures? (10 points)

The Professor does not tell them not to be silly or not to tell lies, but he believes their whole story. He predicts that they will go back to Narnia again, but not through the wardrobe.

Rubric and Points Possible:
Answer __/ 4 pts.; Capitalization __/ 2 pts.; Punctuation __/ 2 pts.; Complete sentences __/ 2 pts.

LWW Final Exam Answer Key

Name ______________________________

Date ______________________________

Vocabulary Matching: Write the letter of the vocabulary word on the line. (10 points)

1. G campaign
2. D quarry
3. A solemn
4. B gaiety
5. J renounced
6. H modest
7. C contentment
8. I treason
9. F enchanted
10. E inquisitive

a. deeply serious and sober
b. high-spirits, merrymaking
c. a feeling of calm or satisfaction
d. a hunted animal; prey
e. curious, or wanting to know more
f. put under a spell
g. a series of operations
h. not drawing attention to your achievements
i. betrayal of country
j. given up something that was yours

Vocabulary Usage: Fill in the blank with the appropriate vocabulary word. (10 points)

appeased	**bane**	**flushed**	**forfeit**	**fraternizing**
gloating	**hoax**	**jeered**	**liberated**	**principal**
reliable	**vermin**			

1. In old times sailors used the North Star for navigating their ships, because it is the most reliable, or dependable, guidepost in the sky.
2. Odysseus was trapped on the island of Calypso, but he was liberated when Hermes convinced her to let him go free.
3. The god Poseidon wrecked Odysseus' boat, and Odysseus had to forfeit his clothes so that he could swim more easily to the shore.
4. The giant Cyclops was the bane of many of Odysseus' men, whom he ate.
5. Odysseus was able to blind the giant, but instead of gloating over the giant and foolishly revealing who he was, he should have immediately run away.
6. When he finally arrived home, he was jeered at by young men because he looked old and poor, and they did not know he was Odysseus.
7. Odyssesus was playing a hoax on the men, and he waited to reveal himself at just the right time.

8. Finally, Odysseus took off his disguise and ___appeased___ his anger at the young men, who had tried to steal his wife and possessions.

9. Odysseus killed all his enemies, including anyone he had seen ___fraternizing___ with the young men.

10. His wife did not believe he was Odysseus at first, and his face ___flushed___ with hurt and anger. In the end, however, she believed him.

Multiple Choice: Circle the best answer for each question. (10 points)

1. The author of *The Lion, the Witch and the Wardrobe* is:
   a. Jr. Tolkien
   b. J. R. R. Tolkien
   c. C. R. Lewis
   (d.) C. S. Lewis

2. The place to which the children go to live is:
   a. a boarding school run by Digory Kirke
   b. a house in London after the war
   (c.) a large house in the country owned by a professor
   d. a castle in the north country of England

3. The Beavers' home is:
   a. a large house in the Wild Wood
   b. a comfortable and cozy cave next door to Tumnus
   (c.) a snug and rustic home on the beavers' dam
   d. a cottage near the Fords of Beruna

4. Mr. Beaver describes Aslan as:
   a. a fierce and wild warrior
   b. the prince of Narnia from over the Sea
   c. the first king of Narnia before the Witch
   (d.) the King of Narnia and the Lord of the whole wood

5. The gifts the children receive are:
   a. a spear, battle axe, bow with arrows, horses to ride on
   b. shield, sword, horn, cordial, and dagger
   c. tea party, sewing machine, fishing gear, sluice-gate
   (d.) shield, sword, bow with arrows, horn, cordial, dagger

6. Because Aslan comes nearer, Narnia is:
   a. in grave peril of fire and water
   b. free from the Witch forever
   c. being decorated with festoons and banners
   (d.) losing its Winter and changing to Spring

7. Aslan arrives with:

   (a.) a great processional of creatures
   b. Father Christmas
   c. no fanfare or celebration since he is humble
   d. the Emperor Beyond the Sea

8. The Emperor is:

   a. Aslan's brother in another world like Narnia
   (b.) the one who put the Deep Magic into Narnia
   c. the one who made the Witch queen and protector of Narnia
   d. a great ruler who lives in the land of Calormen

9. The nicknames Peter, Susan, Edmund, and Lucy get as kings and queens are:

   a. Peter the Brave, Susan the Beautiful, Edmund the Wise, and Lucy the True
   b. Peter the Magnificent, Susan the Beautiful, Edmund the Just, and Lucy the True
   (c.) Peter the Magnificent, Susan the Gentle, Edmund the Just, and Lucy the Valiant
   d. Peter the Brave, Susan the Gentle, Edmund the Wise, and Lucy the Valiant

10. The White Stag is:

   (a.) a stag that would give you wishes if you caught him
   b. a guide to other worlds
   c. a sign of Aslan's return
   d. a royal messenger for the kings and queens of Narnia

Comprehension Short Answer: Answer each question or fill in the blanks. (10 points)

1. Lucy is miserable for several days following her adventure because her siblings thought she was telling a silly lie.
2. The effect the Turkish Delight has on Edmund is that he got hooked on it.
3. When the Beaver speaks of Aslan, Peter feels brave, Susan feels pleasant, Edmund feels horror, and Lucy feels giddy.
4. Edmund betrays the others by telling the Witch the location of the others and their plan to meet Aslan.
5. The sign that the Witch is losing her power is the appearance of Father Christmas.
6. The Deep Magic from the Dawn of Time gave the Witch the right to claim traitors and punish them with death, or else all Narnia will perish / fall / etc.
7. The Witch came to imagine herself as Queen because she was the Emperor's hangman.
8. According to the Deeper Magic, when a victim who has committed no crime is killed in a traitor's stead, the Table will crack and death will start working backwards.

9. The significance of the statues coming to life is that it reinforces the fact that Aslan conquered and reversed death.

10. Mr. Beaver explains that Aslan left quietly because he is not a tame lion.

Composition: (10 points each)

1. Write from dictation the paragraph in Chapter 3 that begins after, "It was a beautiful face in other respects, but proud and cold and stern."

The sledge was a fine sight as it came sweeping toward Edmund with the bells jingling and the dwarf cracking his whip and the snow flying up on each side of it.

Rubric and Points Possible:
Capitalization __/ 2 pts.; Punctuation __/ 2 pts.; Correct words __/ 6 pts.

2. Compare Edmund's reaction to the Beaver's conversation about Aslan to the reaction of the other children. Why do you think he reacts in this way?

While the others have pleasant feelings about Aslan, Edmund's reaction is negative, because the talk of Aslan makes him uncomfortable. Edmund had given in to the temptations of the Queen, which has separated him from Aslan's goodness. He is probably feeling guilty and perhaps fearful that his action will be judged.

Rubric and Points Possible:
Answer __/ 4 pts.; Capitalization __/ 2 pts.; Punctuation __/ 2 pts.; Complete sentences __/ 2 pts.